# Ripples over dreams

Manuel Tenorio Fenton

BookLeaf Publishing

India | USA | UK

*This work is dedicated to my caring family and the friends that I have found along the path.*

# Acknowledgement

I want to thank the reader. Hope these words shed light into your own adventure.

# Preface

This book could be divided into three parts. The first nine poems; *Ripples over dreams and Verses I - VIII* deal with oneiric images, inhabited by Jungian archetypes. Very much like a dream itself, the poems leave a strong impression throughout a sequence of rapidly changing sceneries, as well as visitations from beloved ones that are no longer beside us in the realm of the living.

The second part, from *Take me back there to Chasing shadows*, takes the wisdom from Poetry applied to the description of dreams to the author's life memories, often giving the chance to do a different, more positive interpretation than the initial one which was affected by the immediate reactive human mechanism. Thus, Poetry signifies a possible way of rewriting one's life guided by the subtle connection between conscious and unconscious minds. The third and final part from *Time to Lake Michigan* is a series of poems translated from their original versions in Spanish.

# Ripples over dreams

Terse irruption— blow
in the waters of sleeping being
sows soft gentle flow,
teary constellations have my sky.

I laid this aquatic blanket
to cover the truth, I live
a half-awakened life to pursue
desires like tidal waves poured into me.

Days-long lasts the sensation,
the certainty of your presence
in this plane, like ripples disperse
through the mirror of a quiet soul.

There is no wind that alters sweet
fleeting new formations of stars,
no fast boats set sail afar
when we meet, no words rain over the sea.

And yet so clear like dawn
your message stays a tune
you whistled, a picture
on the surface you have drawn.

# Verses I

I thought of a dream in autumn,
with a cypress that leaned, cracking
dreaming of plucking a star out of the water,
and the wind sings and dances mean
through hay walls, clay falters,
but resists the cotton ice reminder
of the cloak that caresses the bareness.
Eyes that pry the falling snow,
bittersweet tale in the bright light distill,
mezcal that we drink in ponder,
a ray of warmth and affliction fills to meet
astral liquid, trace of petrified oceans,
witness of the tides in full reflection
the star wants to be watched in wonder.

# Verses II

As a stranger, I describe rain falling,
towering appears proud, unveiled mountain,
and the white shade pours but phantom
shadows,
floating torrents tear flows, wet mites of time
in a lone fade blows a silver cover,
lower wind that pretends to recover light,
blind illusions built frostbite in the cold
morning.
As a tourist around a nest flies
miles the keen, abound landscapes to see,
and those who saw the fledgling go,
no coward in flight told their tale
or a rude word called preying on,
and the mountain remains long after
catching fond curtains floating at noon.

# Verses III

Ache that, as soon as comes, teaches
the slow, impertinent pain of age
and so it is no longer a man who is master
but the time; so thick is the mold,
and yet a bell chimes in a fortress
hidden away, walls of quiet air
only care for the flash that yields the storm.
It happens again, the prism of rain
showers that good old cobblestone,
and gone is the scent of flowers
in the downpour, in the deafening tone
just before the calm, just barely aware—
like a hunted hare, like the fog
during early hours with a rising sun.

# Verses IV (Nova)

Wood in its nightly attire
won't burn a secret fire from soot,
hissing ash, slightly ashamed,
too old to utter a shine,
will flame all the same:
pure coal and hardened mineral,
turned airborne sandy and fine.
Words spelled out in gelid air fades
thin code so brief and frail
a tale told to the ages that behold
one breath waging war against the starry
night,
the weather in its rage and might, is
withdrawn,
with smoke in the hurricane eye
and a hidden cry in the clouds that spoke.

# Verses V

Why sometimes the better tides come
when the boat rides the sands,
and the winds throw away but scraps
to the shore, looking for the sun,
long gone to battle its own fight,
for wee hours thaw that glitter
rainbows in its glorious advance.
Sand of the good kind hides deep
along the whipped shore, ever brave
and tall with dunes that seep
golden dust, a spark leaked by greedy wave
will mostly find submarine dark hall
but a fine song sings in the sunset light
the little that stays, ever so mighty and small.

# Verses VI

Dove-like feather fell, cloud holds
its breath and it is an orange show
in heaven's breast, lest one's love goes
deep whether the sun shines or not,
cumulus lit in fire ties the knot
a blast, crimson snow has left
cinders to hover on for the step.
Sought silver light so bright
encore, sickle with a mist
veils the thunder blight, wet fist
lays helpless secret in the bed
of countless storms, the skies
fail to obey and bow, bent a row
of colorful lanes, of treasured sight.

# Verses VII

Yellow whirl, a picture swallows,
of autumn leaves a fallen tree weeps
mellow fill off oaken hollows,
memory moss, green branch tears
flushed images like tossed spore
in hushed forest deeps,
in nature that sleeps and hears.
Colored tulip blossoms in ice,
so nice between crystal gleam
reflections reading every single section
of its petals, the blooming odds
shine fires in the cold metals
that gaze above, amazed
with their own minuscule size.

# Verses VIII

Down the streets smiles holding
the bouquet that I dreamed of giving,
a lady walking on tired stone tiles
as I saw, forgiving a random meet
at evening tea, we are happy
but lament that the silence was faster
and collected our whispers as fees.
Cotton fiber fantasies brushed
in fine hairs, cosmic ray dissects
with all its colors and desired button,
flower of thought, its perfume cares
to blush and snare the bird of spring
and tempest crow all the same,
knows shiny days and darkest nights.

# Take me back there

Let us go to the hallways of an elementary
school,
when they looked so roomy as to hold
illusions,
to the fresh morning hours carrying
typewriters on our shoulders
and ancient ruins illuminated in surrounding
mountains.
Small potatoes in vinegar with chili await
just after the bell rings, for those of quiet stay
and for those looking for trouble and who
run
three hundred steps to the corner and back
after a fist fight.

Take me back to a friend's heartbreaking
confession
and to the humility of washing the feet of
your crush,
to the awkwardness of feeling awkward
among awkward people in the cafeteria
and the mantra of the Holy Father in a
Catholic school.
To the passage of the park where I gave my
first kiss
just to find out later countless generations did
the same there,
and to the euphoria after realizing I was out
of high school
and away from a jackal of a book keeping
teacher.
To the feeling of being chosen to learn science
at the maximum house of studies of the
nation,
and the mystique of teachers with a love to
teach
unveiling secrets while reality unraveled
outside of the circle.

# Oil Paint

Grey in blue diluted for a cloud,
with solvent that smells so loud,
it fills the room, along with the glue,
pasting the light to a sunset west due.

Green hues divide regent flowers,
in infinite gardens, limited views
guide our eyes between colorful powers,
trapped in window sights, tight and loose.

Oily night closes on a faded face,
timeless expression fights to leave a trace
of a man that poses in disguised tension,
only to make his hesitation immortal.

# To camp next to a water stream

Feel your toil be washed away
slowly with the sound of the water
that flows trusting its path to the ocean.
Different, unknown murmurs reveal
a new face of the sleeping forest
when the law of the small creatures begins.
All around you, countless memorable lives are lived
by beings that shout their existence
in the crackle of a branch or a fall of a leaf.
Now the stream has also taken your consciousness,
and the song of the crickets is all that is
below the gentle lull of the trees.

# Road trip

Down goes the road beneath us,
I am surrounded by friends.
Laughter and stories beside me,
a journey that never quite ends.

Skies stretch wide above our way,
we travel as free as the breeze,
and even daylight hours seem to stay
dancing entertained in nearby trees.

What starry night awaits ahead
to frame a glorious moment at the beach,
where the sand is our soft bed
and an everlasting feeling is within reach.

Sometimes I imagine we are still tripping
and decided to go on different paths.
The echoes of footsteps slowly slipping
claimed by the sea and the past.

We had so little, we packed a ton
on top of a Volkswagen beetle with rope,
but we were so young and not alone,
and together we lit the road with hope.

# About a swim in a lake

It was a warm summer day
in the clear lake, I swam across,
kissed by the sun in golden display,
blinding my fears to a split second loss.

Floating on a feeling of freedom,
I belonged for an instant there,
but it was just the lake, calm and unworried,
It was just me breathing the summer air.

Sparkling memory of a brief embrace
by pure nature lured me to scout
the same place, but found no trace
fellow people like me are full of doubt.

A summer lake with arms wide open,
we are free to accept and to give,
from those who know nature and to the
broken,
who have forgotten her and have to live.

# Reflections

Can't help but think when a quirk happens
and mildly diverts the sequence of events,
of whatever higher intelligence or fate
arranged for facts so to occur,
so that I could enjoy yet another orange
sunset
or a long pointless talk with my father in
calm.
Be reminded to let go of the illusion of
control
is the hardest, to surrender in the soft stream
of life that takes us to uncharted landscapes
that we cannot revisit ever again and be
present in a fleeting moment of bliss.
And while it might start raining again
inside my apartment, I decide to thank
for having a place to live in, put the tea pot
on the stove and make some tea
writing these lines that you are now reading.

# White Moth

White Moth dresses fine in a robe like a
bride,
elegant as she glides through the twilight air,
with mystery only by her side,
will choose tonight with whom to pair.

Sweet scents tell a story in the streets,
where she flew without direction,
because no one knows who she meets
in loud bars and intersections.

The moon is her go-to lover
when she can't find a together
the time of passion is over,
towards the sky flies forever.

White Moth desire is not gone
he is just distracted and amiss.
Please wear again your gorgeous gown,
and fly for him to make you his.

# Horizons

Keep the excitement of adventure
when exploring a new country
and wandering around the world.
Far are the times of stillness
into the future and into the past
and all that is left is adaptation.
Thank your shelter because it has kept you
in times of storm and illness
and we all shall continue our path and leave.
Walk in your dream again around the house
with a view of the Pacific Ocean
and listen to the noise of the waves.
One day when you finally make your way
there
everything will seem like a beautiful
excursion
to the horizons that educated our untamed
souls.

# Canoe

Paddle through marshes in silence,
not to waken the crocodile,
whose eyes gleam beneath the surface,
still as stones in the murky isle.

Let the reeds mark subtle contours
of the pathway to the middle,
where the search ends and your truth pours
from a spring with a curious twiddle.

Bushy labyrinth brings you away,
but you row resisting the heat,
to the lead, as far as it may,
as deep under the darkened peat.

Eyes of scaled horror, yellow gems,
will witness your small canoe advance
and get stuck in muddy stems,
turning around in a cautious dance.

# Napping in the tropic

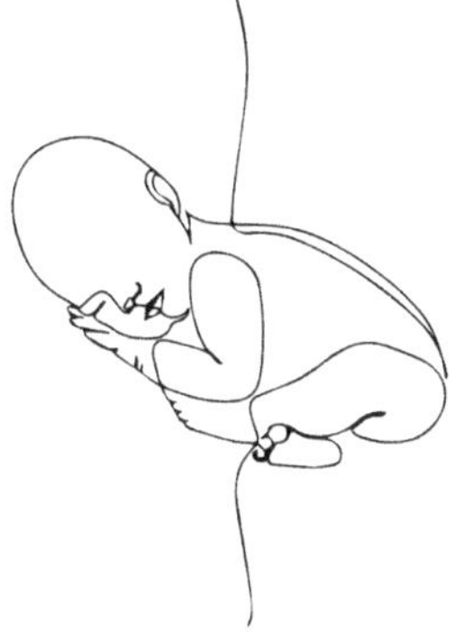

It is around time for my next nap,
my hammock rocks slightly,
and the warm air invites me to rest.
Crickets maintain a cacophony of speeches,
and cicadas answer in the distance
with their own political chants.
No specific tiredness brings me to rest,
it is just the tropic embrace
that demands passive obedience.
Maybe a dream of a lush garden
and a welcoming smile await me
once I have closed my eyes and lay down.
Take your tropical naps seriously;
everyone knows the mosquito bites
when the sun is either settling or rising.

# Chasing shadows

Once I was accused to be shadow-like
or a ghost, I don't really remember,
it was time to work the field with the pike
and plow with the harrow until tender.

Once my passion lamp lacked enough oil
to burn so bright through a drunken man's
night,
it was time to clean the bulb for the coil
that beats in my heart with gentle pure light.

Perhaps our better selves cast a long shade,
a mirage, from an overlapping plane
right here just enough for our souls to bade
and leave us feeling better but the same.

Perhaps in that same instant we became
another being, one that we dared to dream
and from another reality came,
since we are all shadows and passionate
beams.

# Time

So faint the dawn, so brief the breeze,
of great questioning answered,
of a bright yet tasteless sunrise,
time that passes without haste.

With the key of the wave in the mist,
it decodes all the tempests,
the scribe, quill of the ages,
a shooting star that died in the foam.

Gray minotaur of understanding,
it devours the bewildered just the same,
and forces the coward to wait for the hour,
and to the usurer, it grants sustenance.

Wavering and oily wick,
it is the premonition that illuminates
the path that, in the void, is but a thread.

A clock that moves backward and foresees,
between worlds, the second hangs in
suspense,
an invented lie that foretells.

# Fragments

1

What you create will always go to infinity,
like turtles in the deep sea
that unconsciously inhabit the tides.
Like searching for another fertile field
to keep you in the ugly battles,
like the turtle that holds the world.
An angry sky frowns,
and higher spheres, unhurried,
remind patiently, "I am your master."
The seas thrown to great heights
barely murmur in the dream
of fleeting ones with pure intentions.

2

Hidden beneath so much meaninglessness,
the master of distractions spies,
from omnipresent ether blessings
emanates libations of the living saint.

But the cruel demon misses the mark,
the peace of each soul is so foreign to him
that beneath the sun, his fate is unknown, as full
as at night, an obsidian sword.
And to the soul, no battle matters,
it is a great joy so it is so light,
the tundra seems a meadow to it,
unspoken words, its northern light.


3


Sudden fold of the dark cloud
by the shadow of your absent gaze,
drought that punishes but also provides.
In the same heat of existence
that in the void would be harsh harvest,
and with your voice, it is suddenly bliss.
A gray moon with polished silver,
crowned with a royal red eclipse,
as one remembers a past dream.
While the sunset, in celebration, abandons
all composure, well inhabited
by a light that pays tribute to the past.

4

Just as the ant tells its story
and the green grass that breaks the ice
has euphoric small glory
like birds in their first flight.
So I enlist for an adventure
like everyone else, and the night reveals
an ally with sword and armor,
an esoteric armory of enchants.
Of faint flame that invites to burn
thoracic box of particleboard,
a finely tuned clock, science that imitates
voice, murmur that inhabits the desolate.


5

A palm of earth, sworn witness
of cats who spy attentively
the seedbed of discovery.
Description of how, in its elements,
an infinitesimal worm, in its last breath,
cuts memory and knowledge in two.
How stealthily it fixes its prey
like an untamable draconian beast

among black stones, the lizard.
A regrettable congregation of crows
cries, its treasure is no trinket,
and the loss is more than probable.


6


Veil, smoke, and mirror conspire,
death of the race, the illusionist
walks the loose ropes that emulate
the commands of a puppeteer.
Consciousness without time, ascending
like an arrow in the sky, halted
at its zenith, suddenly doubting
the mark it was grateful for.
Beast and hunter cannot help but delight,
infinitely dying and hunting,
losing and winning until exhaustion
like threads intertwined in woven fabric.


7


The inert shell speaks to the void,
a worthy skull of the bronze ages
that time without matter and energy

could not reach, now it enjoys
the darkness, the cold secret
of oblivion that wounds memory.
Good reward of countless stars
carefully named, they call
the armor of a hero without flaws,
protect him from the assault, which they plot,
legend to the one who knows them beautiful
by day
and in the desert night, loves them.


8


Sunlight that continues its trail,
a world in shadow, the same distance
that a seagull accompanies a ship
that the foamy water scrapes with patience
in open sea, a naive straying
of the blue sky in sweet madness.
A myriad of opaline galaxies,
Proteic chains organized
in the frog's egg, giving birth
to the memory of scaled heights,
to a scattered or fine rain,
imagined lives of water beings.

9

Red, buried fused quartz
in vapor, it cries wind's tears,
crystal-clear glass of ages
is granted that settles slowly.
Magma, medium of terrible
and renewing caress, force that heals
the earth, the tangible blessing
of a stony chalice from which life emanates.
Minimalistic seed in its path
defies the silent desert
of absence, the arid path
sown by earlier seeds.

10

Serenity and patience of sand,
of seas of wisdom in their waves
of imperishable light, winged
parts of the whole that stop time.
Docile pale descendant of frost
under the moon, imperceptible presence,
in the dim sky, the luminescence

of stars and their slow march.
Light cohabits in each perplexed flake
by the reflection of constellations,
in pure geometrical progressions,
blue future and crimson past.

11

The same blade of grass that ignites the
prairie
parts in the dark cave the cold shadow,
a splinter that lights up and glows
and harvests the sparks of a bonfire.
On the witness of corroded bronze
the oblivion gnaws mercilessly
the word, a treaty of concord
in the language of a lost people.
And at the level of ants, the grass
cuts the light into vengeful shadows,
like a thousand moons casting elusive
eclipses in the vast infinite.

12

The whistle of silver in the air guides me

to the coast where the foam that withdraws
lives,
and immediately it's mine
the possession of all, like a feather
fall, like light on a journey
caressing the mountains in the mist.
Like a mountain range that fades
in a storm and steep slopes
softened with frequent waters,
the woman who is the earth where she grows,
curves over the sleeping horizon
bathed by the dying lightning.


13


The pebble that sinks with assurance
produces no sound or bubble
nor does it feel the force that pushes it,
depths that it carries on its back.
In heights that only brave ones dare,
the bird gives thanks, and immediately stalks
its prey while taking advantage
of the torrential wind that lifts it.
Words that are lowly and winged,
words are either bird or lifeless pebble

that sail aboard a fortunate flight
toward their own ascent.


14 (NYC)


Eagle molds wings of granite
among rivers of timelessness,
a ship in boarding lets out its cry
from an island in a fleeting world
in currents of the infinite,
from its stone and its messenger truth.
In flight, it finds a sister from the same nest
and they contemplate each other as
suspended,
but when they fall through the sky, struck
down,
they recount battles, and the wind defeated
counts stars woven in the dome
as it turns once more around the sun.


15


Wood that infuses the ocean
intoxicates waves with forbidden alcohols,
a celestial body that doesn't fall in vain

fills the lost eyes with omens.
Illusion that remains impregnable
against all attacks and clings to the world,
to a soul that offers a kind word
and practices its breath on the earth.
Scenes, images on the reverse
of life attest to the inevitable coming
of the softest curtain,
which is the sea in the darkened night.


16


Ice among embers, the ash tries
to record the fire in its course,
its trail declares its ethereal path,
a comet reveals its flight.
A solitary place, what depths
populate the gazes of the absent
like leaves of interfering trees,
like still water wells between ages.
The only reflection of a tide
counts lost quartz among the sands,
like dreams polished by time,
trapped in the net of the swollen moon.

17

A dry leaf becomes dust and fragrance,
a taste, salt from the treasured desert,
light, clarity that for a moment tames
a cornered symphony of color.
An oak burned in sweet flame
slow like resin that crystallizes
a tear, a spirit that bursts
white silk through the omitted atmosphere.
A flame-lit wave is orange as it passes
sweeping incandescent foam
across the dunes of dreams, and gently
feeds the indulgent dawn.

18

Dune that receives the tide
melts in watery pleasures,
without form, it goes wherever it pleases,
accompanied by ephemeral escorts.
A bird of the night in its sweetness
dances, the shadow is its gift and trace
marking mineral veins in its embrace
and hatching in obsidian darkness.

And in the shadows of anonymity
the harshest jaws are silenced maidens,
fighting to the death, miniature beasts
ruthless, indifferent in their dealings.


19


A drop of water that seduces hues
and aligns into an icicle of ice,
leading the battle of colors
in its cold caress that stirs wakefulness.
A frozen facet, the vendetta
crafted, a trick agreed upon by the cold
in the perfect snowflake that challenges
the light to imitate crystallized reality.
A diamond head that strives
over the soft colors of autumn,
an oak lover of its own flame
saves its offspring from pain.


20


Ghost, a sheet of dawn woven
by a loom that stretches seconds
in sweet synapses, a thread that carries

the weight of a protected illusion.
A patch, silk worn by life
that delicate mending lifts
in the air of dreams, enchanting
the portrait of the beloved person.
A white visitor guiding my affairs,
dressed in clouds, no longer scares me,
in the veil of the sky where it seeks
that for a moment we fly together.


21


A lagoon forgives in its reflection
the confused sky, the still air
that filled with everything and nothing
no longer asks for a verb or subject.
Suggested in a whisper, a caress
lifting pure gold in the desert
from the dunes, skillfully erasing
the proof of its passing like a meteor.
But the moon, with grace, gives way,
retreats gently with the tide
and returns anew and strong when it can
to the beach that welcomes and desires it.

# Intercepted Lightning

Fragmented, the dark falls into pieces,
compromised black sky,
from the full moon a lament is heard
and from cold its essence falls, it shivers.

It writhes drunken, red among pleasures,
the needle marking the approach
to the river of disappearance,
sailing, a vigilant candle.

Riding the impulses that once
made you chase the northern wind,
almost convulsing, breathless,
singing out of mind its desires.

Cloud, its testimony has drawn
the naked earth, black ink
exhibited before time, overexcited.

And the second reveals pure intention,
claiming that delayed lightning
domesticated and of caricature.

# Space Rocket

Its limbs governed by weightlessness,
speed and thrust predict
the launch that culminates in orbit,
I jot down the contents below.

The shine of a well-cut diamond
that I recently saw in a museum,
with insistence, I still see it
shining in the spilled rainbow.

The willow leaves still dance
in an oceanic and green meadow,
I stretch over the water like wood
and float wherever the tide leads me.

Burning such selected fuel,
two simple and light memories
I transcend a world of abject paper.

With a couple of well-curated memories
a stratospheric bolide ejects me
when they are already written and forgotten.

# Lord of the Forest

Renewed in the celestial vault
between the clouds, a compartment
where words of value are kept
and coexist in a wild state.

Humble upon witnessing, excited
the edge of the cumulus polished
by the sun, hidden in each flower
and placed perfectly in each petal.

Proven that this tree is not just any tree,
the being we sought presents itself,
a beautiful lesson that illuminates and
encourages,
a glimpse of the plane where it operates.

Suddenly, astonished, it seems to me
I feel the beating of a fertile womb
in every moss sprout that grows.

On the branches of memory, my guilt
dies like an ephemeral insect
in the niche that life sculpts for it.

# Desk Lamp

This light that has come to meet me
and boasts of a new, envied existence
that has no misplaced relevance
which it has obtained by its sudden use.

Now it brings light to my ten tasks:
I must revive some friendships
that await a message with truths,
I must seek some beloved ones.

And in the end, I certainly do nothing,
what I need are two mezcals
to fix the ills this way
and leave my forgotten mission aside.

My lamp wobbles, but it's enough for me
for the hour of divine laziness,
the tide of silence that drags me.

For my life is not behind the showcase
of a very expensive store,
like a fetus I saw under yellowish light.

# San Jose del Pacifico

Night air fluttering
that drives an imperceptible wind,
my skin does not know what I feel
nor my good eye what I see.

In a continuous, quiet murmur
the synchronicity is revealed to me
of a perfect geometry,
to brighten my day off.

I lost my loves in a well,
in a breeze are the stories,
in a bet the memories
and in the greenery are the colors.

Rest your burdens on the earth,
and die today a pleasant death
of who you are and your ways.

Trade for a life in sorrow,
all the water that goes to the seas,
moth to the full moon.

# Axolotl

I watched you conjuring mistakes
while you were hunting me,
by day burning jungles
and by night assembling flowers.

A man standing watching a frieze,
a graphic of his own death
because in living, he ran with luck
throwing paradise down the drain.

In sudden silent violence
deaf to the parrot that refutes,
and blind, you changed your path
insensitive to the raw sap.

It was a drunk misunderstanding
that the perfumed current,
unknowingly, attracted us.

It was false beneath your gaze,
my sometimes lost wandering,
my petrified smile.

# Lake Michigan

Immaterial, albino sunset
with apparent good intentions,
on the margins of foreign stories
and on the margins of an opaline iceberg.

The longed-for spring fosters
the flow of my crystalline life,
the migratory bird approaches
the thaw of this, my hard wait.

And though these cold waves I would avoid,
my whole world would freeze,
on the other shore, as cold or colder,
and in dreams, I would walk the path.

It is time to search in this sphere
for that best-rounded pebble,
the elusive, lasting freedom.

I do not even seek to fill a gap
nor would I change a stone if I could
from the edge of this illuminated lake.